AN "APOSTOLIC EXHORTATION" IS, SIMPLY PUT, A TYPE OF COMMUNICATION from the pope that encourages Christians—and all peoples—to live a certain way and to respond to specific challenges.

In this case, Pope Francis is focusing on what it means in our day and age to fully live the gospel of Jesus Christ. He offers a resounding appeal to live it with joy and fidelity and to "go forth" giving witness to the saving love of Jesus Christ, especially among the poor and marginalized in our world. Pope Francis says over and over that when we serve the least ones among us, we will experience God's incredible love and joy.

Here we invite you to walk with Pope Francis for thirty days, reflecting on his writings in *The Joy of the Gospel*. On each of these pages we also offer a related Scripture passage, a prayer, and a practice in response to the pope's message. May this booklet inspire you to live the gospel as never before, and may it fill your heart with the joy that comes with true discipleship.

CONTENTS

The Scripture quotes were chosen by Gwen Costello, who also wrote the prayers and practices. Cover photo: © Stefano Spaziani
Copyright © 2014 Twenty-Third Publications, a division of Bayard;
One Montauk Avenue, New London, CT 06320. 860-437-3012 or 800-321-0411,
www.23rdpublications.com. No part of this publication may be reproduced in any manner without prior written permission of the publisher. All rights reserved.
ISBN 978-1-62785-020-9 ■ Printed in the U.S.A.

Third Printing 2014

1 | NO ROOM IN OUR HEARTS

*When we get caught up in our own interests
and concerns, we no longer have room in our hearts
for others, no place for the poor. We forget the quiet
joy of God's love.*

SCRIPTURE

Rejoice with those who rejoice, weep with those
who weep. Live in harmony with one another.
Romans 12:15~16

PRAYER

O beloved God, if I have closed my heart to you,
please open it wide that I might reach out beyond
my own interests and concerns to be aware of the
needs of others, especially the poor. Your Son Jesus
became one with all those who have little of this
world's goods, and he proclaimed your kingdom to
them first of all. Make my heart like his, dear God.
Amen.

PRACTICE

Today I will think about Pope Francis' words and try
to let them touch my heart.

2 | A PERSONAL INVITATION

I invite all of you who follow Jesus, wherever you are, to spend time every day renewing your personal relationship with him, letting him touch your hearts.

SCRIPTURE

As the Father has loved me, so I have loved you. Abide in my love. *John 15:9*

PRAYER

Loving God and Father, open my mind and heart to the realization that Jesus is one of the greatest gifts in my life. You invite me through him to a new way of seeing and loving. Beginning today, I will try to be more conscious that Jesus loves me and abides with me, and I will try to renew my relationship with him in all I do today. Amen.

PRACTICE

Today I will set aside a space in my home, if only a small corner, where I can light a candle as a reminder that Jesus abides in me, here and now, and always.

3 | A CALL TO REJOICE

The gospel invites us to rejoice always because it reveals the radiant glory of Christ's cross.

SCRIPTURE

I have said these things to you so that my joy may be in you, and that your joy may be complete. *John 15:11*

PRAYER

Beloved God, I admit to seeing the message of the gospel as difficult and burdensome. I forget that it is meant to be "good news," the announcement that you are with me always, loving me, guiding me, inviting me to incredible joy. Help me to experience the joy of your presence today in all my activities at home and at work. Amen.

PRACTICE

I will try to focus on the things in life that give me joy today, especially God's gift of Jesus Christ, and I will try to share this joy with everyone I encounter.

4 | WHERE JOY ABIDES

I can say that the most beautiful and natural expressions of joy I have ever seen in my life were in poor people who had little to hold on to in their lives.

SCRIPTURE

I was hungry and you gave me food; I was thirsty and you gave me something to drink. I was a stranger and you welcomed me. *Matthew 25:35*

PRAYER

Beloved God, if the very poor know how to live the gospel, to feed one another, to quench one another's thirst, to welcome the stranger, I too should respond to this call of Jesus. My desire for comfort and order keeps me from seeing and imitating those who have little of this life's goods. Change my heart, O God. Amen.

PRACTICE

Today I will try to be aware of the very poor in our world, to pray for them, and to try to help them in some small way.

5 | HOW GOODNESS SPREADS

Goodness always tends to spread, and as it expands it takes root and grows. With every authentic act of goodness, we experience an inner freedom that makes us more sensitive to the needs of others.

SCRIPTURE

But the fruit of the Spirit is love, joy, peace, forbearance, kindness, goodness, faithfulness, gentleness, and self-control. *Galatians 5:22~23*

PRAYER

Dear Holy Spirit, fill my heart with all your gifts and in particular the gift of goodness. Help me to be more aware of the needs of others and to reach out with genuine love, that I might experience the kind of inner freedom you promise. Open my heart as well to all the other gifts you have implanted in my heart. Amen.

PRACTICE

I will begin this very day to think of ways I can love and serve others with goodness, and I will try to reach out to one particular person at home or at work.

6 | DON'T BE GLOOMY!

When you live the gospel, don't look like you have just come back from a funeral! Don't give in to discouragement or impatience, but open your hearts to the joy of Christ.

SCRIPTURE

Rejoice in the Lord always. I will say it again: Rejoice!
Philippians 4:4

PRAYER

Loving God, if I think about it, I realize that I never pray for the gift of joy. I have become discouraged and impatient about many things in my life, and after reading Pope Francis' words, I know that I need to spend more time "opening my heart to the joy of Christ." I want and need to listen to the words of the gospel and let them really touch me at the deepest level of my life. Help me, please, to do this. Amen.

PRACTICE

I will spend time in my prayer space today, asking God to give me the "joy of Christ."

7 | GOD OFFERS EVERYTHING

*When we make the effort to return to Jesus
and recover the original freshness of the gospel,
we find new ways of being creative. Though God
asks everything of us, he also offers everything to us.*

SCRIPTURE

Come, you who are blessed by my Father, inherit the kingdom prepared for you. *Matthew 25:34*

PRAYER

The pope seems to be saying, dear God, that living the gospel is both difficult and rewarding. God asks everything of me and gives me everything. Though it might take more time and attention than I am sometimes willing or able to give, I do want to focus on what Jesus is saying in the gospel. I would like to recover the "original freshness" of truly knowing him. Help me find my way. Amen.

PRACTICE

I will focus today on the graces God gives me rather than on the difficulties of the call to follow Jesus.

8 | EVERYONE'S INVITED

The joy of the gospel is for all people: no one can be left out. We all have the duty to share this joy and invite others to "the delicious banquet" of knowing Jesus Christ.

SCRIPTURE

There will be more joy in heaven over one sinner who repents than over ninety-nine righteous persons who need no repentance. *Luke 15:7*

PRAYER

O beloved God, I want to experience this "delicious banquet" myself and to know the joy of the gospel. I am distracted by my own interests and concerns, and I find it hard to believe in the kind of joy the pope describes. I do want to rediscover it and then share it with my family, friends, and coworkers. Open my heart anew to your Son's gospel words. Amen.

PRACTICE

I will spend time today reflecting on today's Scripture verse, mainly on the word "joy."

9 | BEAUTIFUL AND GRAND

We should share what is most beautiful, most grand, most appealing about Christ's gospel and at the same time what is most necessary. Before all else, it invites us to respond to the God of love who saves us.

SCRIPTURE

Ask and you will receive, so that your joy may be complete. *John 16:24*

PRAYER

Loving God, Jesus prayed for his followers at the last supper that they might have complete joy, and he encouraged them to "ask" for it. The pope encourages me to share the joy of my faith and the "beauty and grandness" of God's love. I ask you to open my heart and mind to these teachings. Please turn my heart of stone into a heart of fire, burning for you, aching for the joy that comes with living the gospel. Amen.

PRACTICE

Five times throughout my day, I will ask Jesus to fill my heart with his joy.

10 | SEEING GOD IN OTHERS

*The gospel invites us to see God in others
and to reach out beyond ourselves to seek the good
of others. This is an invitation that cannot be
ignored or obscured!*

SCRIPTURE

I give you a new command: Love one another. Just
as I have loved you, you must also love one another.
John 13:34

PRAYER

Sometimes, dear God, I feel that I have no room in
my life for "others." And yet Jesus clearly teaches that
I should love others as he has loved me. Pope Francis
tells me that the invitation to do good for others is
essential for Jesus' followers. Help me to understand
and accept these teachings, that I might reach out
beyond myself to think of others first. Amen.

PRACTICE

I will take one small step today toward loving and
serving others at home, at work, or in my community.

11 | TOUCHED BY GOD

Everyone needs to be touched by the comfort and attraction of God's saving love, which is mysteriously at work in each of us, above and beyond our faults and failings.

SCRIPTURE

If you are in Christ, you are a new creation; the old has gone, the new has come! *2 Corinthians 5:17*

PRAYER

May your saving love touch me, O God, at the deepest level of my being. The Holy Father assures me that you are guiding me in spite of my faults and failings, and that you are always mysteriously at work in me. Give me faith that I might believe this with all my heart and then be able to touch all those around me with the "comfort and attraction" of your saving love. Amen.

PRACTICE

I will repeat often today: "If I am in Christ, I am a new creation."

12 | THE GOSPEL IMPELS US

The gospel impels us to share its good news, not so much with friends and wealthy neighbors, but above all with the poor, the sick, and the marginalized.

SCRIPTURE

Invite to your banquet those who cannot repay you: the poor, the crippled, the lame, and the blind.
Luke 14:13

PRAYER

I am hearing this, loving God, as if for the first time. You ask me to share my life and my possessions with those who can't repay me and even invite them into my home! I have a long way to go in sharing myself in this way. I need you to dispel my selfish impulses and build up in me the virtues of generosity and goodness. Transform me, O God, and open my heart to your good news. Amen.

PRACTICE

I will try to think of one way today to share the good news with the poor, the sick, or the marginalized.

13 | NOT ON THE NEWS

*How can it be that it's not on the news when
an elderly homeless person dies of exposure,
but it is news when the stock market loses two
points? This is a clear case of exclusion!*

SCRIPTURE

I was naked and you gave me clothing; I was sick and
you took care of me. *Matthew 25:36*

PRAYER

I feel the pinch, or better yet, the punch of Pope
Francis' words, dear God. He's so right. The news
tends to focus on the wealthy, the successful, the
beautiful. What about that elderly homeless person?
Jesus makes it so clear that he expects us to care for
the hungry, thirsty, naked, and sick. My life is so far
from this ideal and thus also far from gospel joy. Give
me courage, O God, to change. Amen.

PRACTICE

I will take time today to think about the pope's
words and how they can change my life.

14 | A CALL TO COMPASSION

Almost without being aware of it, we are incapable of feeling compassion for the poor, weeping for other people's pain, or feeling a need to help them.

SCRIPTURE

But the Helper, the Holy Spirit, whom the Father will send in my name, will teach you all things and help you remember all that I have said to you. *John 14:26*

PRAYER

I am reminded anew, Holy Spirit, that you want me to live for others, especially the poor, and you want me to "weep for other people's pain." When I look deep into my heart, I recognize how numb I am to this call, how I have indeed become incapable of feeling compassion for Jesus' least ones. Holy Spirit, my helper and guide, help me to remember how to be compassionate. Amen.

PRACTICE

I will spend time in my prayer space today asking that I might have compassion and love for the poor.

15 | DON'T LET THIS HAPPEN!

*Sadly, even many with solid doctrinal and spiritual
convictions are seeking power and human glory
rather than the good of others. Don't let this happen
to you! Keep your missionary spirit.*

SCRIPTURE

See that none of you repays evil for evil, but always
seek to do good for one another. Remember to keep
the fire of the Spirit burning. *1 Thessalonians 5:15, 19*

PRAYER

Pope Francis is teaching me, O God, that even when
I believe every word of the Creed and even when
I profess that spiritual values and practices are of
great importance, my heart might still be untouched
by the needs of those around me. Help me to move
from head to heart with my beliefs, that I might
keep alive "the missionary spirit" that impels me to
help others. Amen.

PRACTICE

I will ponder today whether I am among the "many"
the pope is talking about.

16 | KEEP COMMUNITY!

*Though we have many frailties, never forget
that Jesus will give us the strength we need to bond
together as believers. Let's not be robbed
of community!*

SCRIPTURE

My grace is sufficient for you, for my power is made
perfect in weakness. *2 Corinthians 12:9*

PRAYER

We followers of Jesus are sometimes a weak and
sorry lot, dear God, but Pope Francis assures us that
Jesus will give us the strength we need—as a community—to experience the joy of the gospel. Help
me to rise to this occasion, to be a follower who em-
braces the teachings of Jesus and gains strength from
my parish community to do good for others, as well
as to profess my faith and join in prayer and worship.
Give me your grace to do these things. Amen.

PRACTICE

I will say five times today: "God's grace is sufficient
for me."

17 | HOLD ON TO LOVE

To pray for someone who irritates you is a beautiful step forward in love and an act of evangelization. Do this today! Don't be robbed of fraternal love!

SCRIPTURE

Forgive us our trespasses as we forgive those who trespass against us. *Luke 11:4*

PRAYER

O loving God, Pope Francis is hitting me where it hurts! He's saying that real love involves both prayer for those I would rather not pray for and true forgiveness, so that I might move on with "fraternal love" in my heart. That's what gospel living calls for, and that's what I want to embrace in my daily life. Give me the grace to do this, O God, starting today. Amen.

PRACTICE

Pray the Our Father often throughout this day. (You can find the biblical versions in the Bible in the gospels of Matthew [6:9–13] and Luke [11:2–4].)

18 | CHRIST LIVES IN US

All of us need to grow in Christ. Living the gospel should increase our desire for this growth, so that we can say wholeheartedly that Christ lives in us.

SCRIPTURE

I have been crucified with Christ. It is no longer I who live, but Christ who lives in me. *Galatians 2:19~20*

PRAYER

I want to grow in Christ, beloved God, and according to Pope Francis, that means delving more deeply into the gospel message. I confess that I hear the Scripture at Mass but don't always pay attention to it. I don't follow up by reading the gospel on my own or reflecting on its meaning for my life. Teach me how to let Christ live in me. Teach me what it means to live the gospel in my life. Amen.

PRACTICE

Today I will write down three ways I can let the message of Jesus touch and change my life.

19 | SOMETHING BEAUTIFUL

Proclaiming Christ is not only right and true
but also something beautiful that fills our lives
with new splendor and profound joy,
even in the midst of difficulties.

SCRIPTURE

Blessed be the God and Father of our Lord Jesus
Christ, who has blessed us in Christ with every spiritual blessing. *Ephesians 1:3*

PRAYER

Dear God, I do have many difficulties in my life, and I
tend to let them distract and even overwhelm me, so
much so that I forget my call to "proclaim Christ." I
really need "something beautiful," and "splendor and
profound joy" in my life, and Pope Francis says this
comes from living the gospel. I want to focus more
on this and learn to do what is "right and true" even
in the midst of the distractions of my daily life. Amen.

PRACTICE

Today I will take one small step toward proclaiming
the values of Christ in my workplace.

20 | AUTHENTIC FAITH

*Authentic faith—which is never comfortable—
always involves a deep desire to change the world,
to transmit values, to leave this earth better
than we found it.*

SCRIPTURE

We do not lose heart...because we look not at what
can be seen but at what cannot be seen, which is
eternal. *2 Corinthians 4:16, 18*

PRAYER

I do believe, loving God, that without your grace I
cannot do the things Pope Francis challenges me to
do. I often lose heart because I forget what is most
important in life: "a deep desire to change the world,
to transmit values, to leave this earth better than
I found it." Give me the authentic faith the pope
describes, and strengthen me to live it with all my
heart, even when it's not comfortable. Amen.

PRACTICE

I will do one thing today (at home, at work, in my
neighborhood) to change the world.

21 | AN ESSENTIAL SIGN

We can't always reflect the beauty of the gospel, but there is one sign we should never abandon: the option for those who are least in our society.

SCRIPTURE

The Samaritan went to him, bandaged his wounds, put him on his own animal, and took him to an inn… "Go and do likewise," Jesus said. *Luke 10:34, 37*

PRAYER

Our whole culture, creator God, focuses on those who have the most and whom society esteems. Pope Francis is asking me to abandon this way of thinking and to reflect the "beauty of the gospel" by turning to the least ones, those whom society discards. I need your grace to begin thinking and acting this way. I do want to reflect the values of Jesus in my daily life. Help me in this difficult effort, O God. Amen.

PRACTICE

I will try to be a Good Samaritan in one small way today.

22 | FOR THE POOR

I want a Church that is poor and for the poor.
People with nothing have so much to teach us.
In their difficulties they experience
the suffering Christ.

SCRIPTURE

Though he was rich, our Lord Jesus Christ became poor for your sakes, so that through his poverty you might become rich. *2 Corinthians 8:9*

PRAYER

This is Pope Francis' dream, O God—that we let go of our attachment to material things and focus on those who have very little of this world's goods. I am so attached to what I have that this prospect makes me nervous and afraid. I need to travel so far to get to a new mindset, and for this I depend on "the grace of our Lord Jesus Christ." He became poor to make me rich in ways beyond my understanding. Amen.

PRACTICE

I will try to learn one lesson today from the poor.

23 | WORDS OF AFFECTION

*If anyone feels offended by my words, know
that I speak them with affection and the best
of intentions. I'm only interested in helping you live
a more humane, noble, and fruitful life.*

SCRIPTURE

I do not cease to give thanks for you as I remember
you in my prayers..., and may you come to know
the immeasurable wisdom and power of God.
Ephesians 1:16, 17, 19

PRAYER

Bless Pope Francis, beloved God, as he seeks to
teach us the way of the gospel. His message is difficult but when lived fully it can be a source of deep
joy. Help me to set as my own goal to live a "more
humane, noble, and fruitful life" through gospel living. Thank you for the prayers Pope Francis prays
for all of us who are trying to follow Christ. Amen.

PRACTICE

I will pray for Pope Francis throughout my day, that
his message might touch many minds and hearts.

24 | LIKE ST. FRANCIS

*Like Saint Francis of Assisi, all of us Christians
are called to watch over and protect the fragile
world in which we live—as well as all its peoples.*

SCRIPTURE

Let the heavens rejoice, let the earth be glad; let the sea
resound, and all that is in it; all will sing before the Lord.
Psalm 96:11~12

PRAYER

Help me to imitate St. Francis, the pope's namesake,
that I might value everything you have created, O
God, and rejoice in it. May I never consciously harm
any living creature or any part of all that you have
created. Teach me how to better watch over and protect this fragile world in which I live. Amen.

PRACTICE

I will learn about "Francis of Assisi" on the Internet
today and reflect on the way he treated created
things.

25 | MY DEEP LONGING

How I long to find the right words to stir up enthusiasm for an evangelization that is full of fervor, joy, generosity, courage, boundless love, and attraction!

SCRIPTURE

Let us not become weary in doing good, for at the proper time we will reap a harvest if we do not give up. *Galatians 6:9*

PRAYER

Creator God, fill my heart with the kind of enthusiasm for the gospel that Pope Francis speaks of, one that is full of so many positive virtues and, most of all, joy. I know that his words of encouragement will not be enough for me, however, unless I allow the fire of the Holy Spirit to burn in my heart. Come, Holy Spirit, and fill me with that fire, and help me to not "grow weary in doing good." Amen.

PRACTICE

Today I will try to practice one of the virtues Pope Francis mentions above.

26 | FOLLOWING THE SAINTS

*We should follow the example of the early Christians
and our many brothers and sisters throughout history
who were filled with joy, unflagging courage,
and zeal in proclaiming the gospel.*

SCRIPTURE

Joyfully give thanks to the Father, who has qualified
you to share in the inheritance of the saints in the
kingdom of light. *Colossians 1:12*

PRAYER

I would love to walk with the saints, dear God, those
who have proclaimed the gospel throughout the
ages "with joy, unflagging courage, and zeal." These
virtues are foreign to me sometimes because I yield
to the discouragement and cynicism of this present
age. Change my heart and open my eyes to all the
ways I can live and share the good news that Jesus
proclaimed. Amen.

PRACTICE

I will pray today for the virtues of joy, courage, and zeal
that I might better proclaim the gospel of Jesus.

27 | EMBRACING ALL

*Moved by Jesus' example, enter fully into
the fabric of society, sharing the lives of all,
listening to their concerns, and helping them
materially and spiritually.*

SCRIPTURE

We are known as sorrowful, yet always rejoicing;
poor, yet making many rich; having nothing, and
yet possessing everything. *2 Corinthians 6:10*

PRAYER

Our Father in Heaven, stir my heart to take the message of Jesus more fully into the "fabric of society,"
especially at work and in my community. May I care
about and share the lives of everyone I encounter,
listen to them, and help them both financially and
spiritually as I am able. This is how Pope Francis is
calling me to follow Jesus. I truly want to do this.
Amen.

PRACTICE

I will take time today to reflect on all the ways I am
already "moved by Jesus' example" in my daily life.

28 | NOT FULLY LIVING

When we hide, refuse to share, stop giving, and lock ourselves up in own comforts, we are not living fully. Such a life is nothing less than slow suicide.

SCRIPTURE

I have learned the secret of being content in any and every situation, whether well fed or hungry, whether living in plenty or in want. *Philippians 4:12*

PRAYER

Loving God, help me to live my life as fully as possible. Pope Francis says fear, selfishness, and preoccupation with my own comforts are keeping me from responding to the call of Jesus and are like "slow suicide." That's certainly not what I want. Like St. Paul in the Scripture verse, I want to be content in "any and every situation" that life offers me. Help me in all these resolves. Amen.

PRACTICE

I will reflect on these strong words of Pope Francis today and judge myself by them.

29 | KEEP MARCHING

*Let us keep marching forward; let us give God
everything, allowing him to make our efforts
bear fruit in his good time.*

SCRIPTURE

May you live a life worthy of the Lord and please
him in every way: bearing fruit in every good work,
growing in the knowledge of God. *Colossians 1:10*

PRAYER

Lord God of all, give me the courage, please, to keep
"marching forward" in an effort to give you everything. May my efforts bear fruit through the good
works I do, and may I grow deeper in my knowledge
of you. All these things are difficult at times, and I
need your grace and guidance to bring them to frui-
tion. May I begin this very day to get back in step
in my march toward you as I embrace a gospel way
of living. Amen.

PRACTICE

I will practice "marching forward" today, one step
at a time.

30 | MARY IS OUR GUIDE

*Mary, Virgin and Mother, help us to bear
radiant witness to generous faith, justice, and love
of the poor, that the joy of the gospel may reach
the ends of the earth.*

SCRIPTURE

I am the handmaid of the Lord; be it done to me according to your word. *Luke 1:38*

PRAYER

Just as Pope Francis looks to Mary as an example of gospel living, so may I, gracious God. May she help me to bear "radiant witness" to my faith, to my practice of justice, and to my love and service for the poor. I want to say to you as Mary did: Be it done to me as you want it done. May I reflect the joy of the gospel in every aspect of my life. Amen.

PRACTICE

I will pray often today: "I am at your service, O God; be it done to me as you will."